Chapter 1: Introduction to Marathon Running

What is a Marathon?

The marathon, a classic long-distance running event, holds a special place in the world of sports and human achievement. Named after the Greek soldier Pheidippides' legendary run from Marathon to Athens in 490 BC to deliver news of victory, the modern marathon distance of 42.195 kilometers (or 26.2 miles) was established during the 1908 London Olympics and has since become a pinnacle of endurance and determination.

History and Evolution

The marathon's history intertwines with tales of heroism, determination, and the human spirit. From its origins in ancient Greece to its revival as a modern Olympic event, the marathon has captured the imagination of athletes and spectators alike. The story of Pheidippides' run during the Battle of Marathon and subsequent impact on the Olympic Games serves as a testament to the enduring legacy of this iconic race.

Significance in Modern Times

In contemporary society, the marathon represents more than just a sporting event; it symbolizes personal challenge, perseverance, and community. Millions of runners around the globe aspire to complete a marathon, pushing their physical and mental limits to achieve a significant personal milestone. Beyond individual goals, marathons often serve as charitable fundraisers, community events, and celebrations of human achievement.

Why Run a Marathon?

Personal Achievement and Growth

Running a marathon is a transformative experience that tests both physical endurance and mental resilience. For many, the journey from non-runner to marathon finisher represents a journey of personal growth, self-discovery, and accomplishment. Crossing the finish line after months of training is a tangible manifestation of dedication and perseverance, instilling a sense of pride and fulfillment that extends far beyond race day.

Health and Fitness Benefits

The physical benefits of marathon training extend beyond cardiovascular endurance. Long-distance running promotes overall fitness by strengthening muscles, improving joint flexibility, and enhancing aerobic capacity. Regular training also supports weight management, reduces stress levels, and boosts immune function, contributing to long-term health and well-being.

Mental Strength and Discipline

Preparing for a marathon requires mental fortitude and discipline. Enduring months of training, overcoming setbacks, and pushing through physical fatigue builds mental resilience and confidence. The marathon journey teaches valuable lessons in goal-setting, time management, and perseverance, equipping runners with essential life skills that extend beyond the realm of running.

Setting Your Goals

Defining Your Motivation

Before embarking on your marathon journey, take time to reflect on your reasons for running. Whether you seek personal challenge, health improvement, or community engagement, clarifying your motivations will guide your training and keep you focused during challenging moments.

SMART Goal Setting

Setting specific, measurable, achievable, relevant, and time-bound (SMART) goals is essential for marathon preparation. Begin by establishing a target race date and desired finishing time, taking into account your current fitness level and training experience. Break down your goal into smaller milestones, such as weekly mileage targets or incremental speed improvements, to track progress and stay motivated throughout your training journey.

Embracing the Journey

While achieving your marathon goal is undoubtedly rewarding, remember that the journey itself holds immense value. Embrace the process of training, learning from setbacks, and celebrating small victories along the way. Building a supportive network of fellow runners, coaches, and mentors can provide encouragement and guidance throughout your marathon preparation, fostering a sense of camaraderie and shared accomplishment.

Takeaway

Embarking on the journey from couch to marathon requires dedication, perseverance, and a willingness to embrace challenges along the way. By understanding the history and significance of the marathon, identifying your personal motivations, and setting SMART goals, you can lay a solid foundation for success in your marathon journey. Embrace the transformative power of long-distance running, celebrate your progress, and embrace the lessons learned throughout your training. In the chapters that follow, we will delve deeper into the practical aspects of marathon preparation, including training strategies, nutrition guidelines, injury prevention, and race day preparation, ensuring that you are well-equipped to achieve your marathon goals.

Chapter 2: Getting Started

Assessing Your Current Fitness Level

Before embarking on your marathon journey, it's essential to assess your current fitness level to establish a baseline and determine your starting point. This evaluation helps tailor your training plan to your individual needs, minimizes the risk of injury, and ensures effective progression towards your marathon goal.

Physical Assessment

Begin by conducting a comprehensive physical assessment to evaluate your cardiovascular fitness, muscular strength, flexibility, and overall health. Consider performing the following assessments:

- **Cardiovascular Fitness:** Conduct a baseline aerobic assessment, such as a timed run or walk test, to gauge your endurance and cardiovascular capacity.
- **Muscular Strength and Endurance:** Assess your muscular strength and endurance through basic exercises, such as push-ups, squats, or planks, to identify areas for improvement and establish a strength training baseline.
- **Flexibility:** Evaluate your flexibility using simple stretches or mobility exercises to identify any tightness or limitations that may impact your running mechanics.

Health Screening

Consult with a healthcare professional, such as your physician or a sports medicine specialist, to undergo a thorough health screening. This assessment helps identify any underlying medical conditions, orthopedic concerns, or risk factors that may affect your ability to participate in marathon training safely. Discuss your medical history, current fitness level, and goals for marathon training to receive personalized recommendations and guidance.

Goal Setting Based on Assessment

Based on your fitness assessment and health screening results, establish realistic and achievable goals for your marathon training journey. Consider factors such as your desired race completion time, incremental fitness improvements, and milestones for tracking progress throughout your training program. Set SMART (Specific, Measurable, Achievable, Relevant, Time-bound) goals to ensure clarity, motivation, and accountability in pursuing your marathon aspirations.

Choosing the Right Shoes and Gear

Selecting appropriate running shoes and gear is essential for optimizing comfort, performance, and injury prevention throughout your marathon training. Investing in quality equipment that meets your individual needs and preferences enhances your running experience and supports long-term success in achieving your marathon goals.

Running Shoes

Choose running shoes that provide adequate cushioning, support, and stability based on your foot type, running mechanics, and training environment. Consider visiting a specialty running store or consulting with a professional shoe fitter to undergo a gait analysis and receive personalized recommendations for selecting the right footwear. Factors to consider when choosing running shoes include:

- **Foot Type:** Determine whether you have a neutral arch, high arch, or flat feet to select shoes that provide appropriate support and alignment.
- **Cushioning:** Choose shoes with sufficient cushioning to absorb impact forces and reduce the risk of overuse injuries during long-distance running.
- **Fit and Comfort:** Ensure a proper fit with ample room in the toe box and snug heel support to prevent blisters, chafing, or discomfort during prolonged running sessions.

Apparel and Accessories

Select lightweight, moisture-wicking apparel designed for running to enhance breathability, comfort, and temperature regulation during training sessions. Consider investing in technical fabrics that wick sweat away from the skin, minimize friction, and provide freedom of movement. Essential running gear and accessories may include:

- **Moisture-Wicking Clothing:** Choose shirts, shorts, and socks made from breathable materials to keep you dry and comfortable throughout your runs.

- **Compression Gear:** Consider wearing compression socks, sleeves, or tights to improve circulation, reduce muscle fatigue, and enhance recovery during and after training.
- **Hydration Systems:** Carry a handheld water bottle, hydration belt, or hydration pack to maintain optimal fluid balance and electrolyte levels during long-distance runs.
- **Reflective Gear:** Wear reflective clothing or accessories to enhance visibility and safety when running in low-light conditions or during early morning or evening sessions.
- **GPS Watch:** Use a GPS-enabled sports watch or smartphone app to track your running distance, pace, and progress, allowing you to monitor performance and adjust training intensity as needed.

Creating a Training Schedule

Developing a structured training schedule is crucial for building endurance, improving performance, and preparing your body for the physical demands of marathon running. A well-designed training program incorporates progressive mileage, varied workouts, adequate recovery, and strategic rest periods to maximize training adaptations and minimize the risk of overtraining or injury.

Training Principles

Understand fundamental training principles to guide the development of your marathon training schedule:

- **Progressive Overload:** Gradually increase training volume (mileage) and intensity (pace) over time to stimulate physiological adaptations, such as improved cardiovascular fitness and muscular endurance.
- **Periodization:** Divide your training program into distinct phases, such as base training, build-up, peak performance, and tapering, to optimize fitness gains and peak performance on race day.
- **Specificity:** Tailor your training regimen to replicate the physiological and biomechanical demands of marathon running, focusing on long runs, tempo runs, speed workouts, and recovery runs to improve endurance, speed, and running economy.

Components of a Training Schedule

Structure your marathon training schedule to include the following key components:

- **Long Runs:** Schedule weekly long runs to progressively increase distance and time on your feet, building aerobic capacity and mental resilience for marathon distance.

- **Speed Workouts:** Incorporate interval training, tempo runs, or fartlek sessions to improve running speed, lactate threshold, and race pace performance.
- **Cross-Training:** Include non-impact activities such as cycling, swimming, or strength training to enhance muscular balance, prevent overuse injuries, and maintain overall fitness.
- **Rest and Recovery:** Allocate dedicated rest days and recovery periods between training sessions to allow for tissue repair, glycogen replenishment, and mental rejuvenation.
- **Tapering:** Implement a tapering phase in the final weeks leading up to race day to reduce training volume while maintaining intensity, allowing for optimal physical and psychological readiness.

Sample Training Plan

Design a sample marathon training plan based on your fitness level, race goals, and available time commitment. Customize your training schedule to accommodate personal preferences, work-life balance, and individual training adaptations. Consider the following template for a beginner marathon training plan:

- **Week 1-4 (Base Training):** Focus on establishing a foundation with easy-paced runs, cross-training activities, and strength exercises. Gradually increase weekly mileage and incorporate core workouts for stability and endurance.

- **Week 5-12 (Build-Up Phase):** Integrate longer weekend long runs, speed workouts (intervals or tempo runs), and cross-training sessions. Gradually increase mid-week mileage and maintain consistency in training intensity.
- **Week 13-16 (Peak Performance):** Reach peak mileage with your longest long run, simulate race-day conditions (nutrition, hydration, pacing) during training runs, and practice mental strategies for race day success.
- **Week 17-18 (Tapering Phase):** Reduce training volume while maintaining intensity with shorter runs, tapering long runs, and incorporating light cross-training activities. Focus on rest, recovery, and mental preparation leading up to race day.

Adjusting Your Plan

Monitor your progress, listen to your body, and adjust your training plan based on feedback from training sessions, recovery indicators, and overall performance. Be flexible in modifying workouts, rest days, or training volume to accommodate fatigue, prevent injury, and optimize training adaptations throughout your marathon preparation.

Takeaway

Getting started on your marathon journey requires thoughtful preparation, commitment to training, and a personalized approach to achieving your goals. By assessing your current fitness level, selecting the right shoes and gear, and creating a structured training schedule, you lay the groundwork for success in building endurance, improving performance, and embracing the challenges of marathon running.

As you progress through your training program, prioritize consistency, patience, and self-care to maximize training adaptations and minimize the risk of overtraining or injury. Listen to your body, seek guidance from experienced runners or coaches, and celebrate milestones and achievements along the way. In the chapters that follow, we will delve deeper into practical strategies for marathon preparation, including nutrition guidelines, injury prevention strategies, mental preparation techniques, and race-day preparations, ensuring that you are well-equipped to embark on the transformative journey from couch to marathon finish line.

Chapter 3: Building Your Base

Building a strong foundation is crucial for marathon training success. This chapter explores the principles of endurance training, the importance of gradually increasing milcagc, and incorporating cross-training and strength training to support your marathon journey.

Understanding Endurance Training

Endurance training forms the cornerstone of marathon preparation, focusing on developing aerobic capacity, muscular endurance, and mental resilience. This section delves into the physiological adaptations that occur during endurance training and outlines key principles to optimize training effectiveness.

Principles of Endurance Training

Endurance training is centered on gradually increasing the body's capacity to sustain prolonged physical activity. Key principles include:

- **Progressive Overload:** Gradually increasing training stimulus (distance, duration, intensity) to elicit physiological adaptations without risking injury or burnout.
- **Specificity:** Tailoring training to mimic the demands of marathon running, emphasizing long runs, steady-state efforts, and race-pace simulations.
- **Individualization:** Customizing training plans based on individual fitness levels, goals, and responses to training stimuli.
- **Periodization:** Structuring training phases (base, build-up, peak, taper) to optimize fitness gains and peak performance on race day.

Benefits of Endurance Training

Endurance training enhances cardiovascular fitness, improves aerobic efficiency, and increases muscular endurance. Benefits include:

- **Improved Oxygen Utilization:** Enhanced ability to deliver oxygen to working muscles, delaying fatigue and improving performance.
- **Muscular Adaptations:** Increased mitochondrial density and capillary network development in muscles, supporting energy production and nutrient delivery.
- **Mental Resilience:** Strengthened mental toughness and ability to cope with physical discomfort and fatigue during long-distance running.

Components of Endurance Training

Effective endurance training encompasses a variety of workouts to build aerobic capacity, enhance endurance, and prepare for the demands of marathon distance:

- **Long Runs:** Weekly long runs progressively increase in distance (mileage) to build physical and mental endurance. These runs simulate race conditions and prepare runners for sustained efforts.
- **Steady-State Runs:** Longer, moderate-paced runs that improve aerobic threshold and teach pacing strategies.

- **Tempo Runs:** Runs at a comfortably hard pace (tempo or lactate threshold pace) to improve speed endurance and tolerance to sustained effort.
- **Recovery Runs:** Short, easy-paced runs or active recovery sessions to facilitate recovery, maintain aerobic fitness, and promote muscle repair.

Start Slow: Building Mileage Gradually

Gradually increasing mileage is essential to prevent injuries, adapt to training stress, and build a solid aerobic base. This section outlines strategies for safely and effectively progressing your weekly mileage throughout your marathon training program.

Mileage Progression Strategies

- **Week-by-Week Increment:** Increase weekly mileage by 10-15% to allow for adaptation and recovery between training sessions.
- **Long Run Progression:** Gradually increase the distance of your weekly long run by 1-2 miles (or more for experienced runners) to build endurance and confidence.
- **Consistent Build-Up:** Maintain consistency in training volume and intensity to avoid sudden spikes in mileage that could lead to overuse injuries.

- **Rest and Recovery:** Incorporate recovery weeks every 3-4 weeks, reducing mileage and intensity to allow for physiological adaptation and mental rejuvenation.

Adjusting Mileage Based on Experience

- **Beginners:** Start with low-to-moderate mileage and prioritize gradual progression to build endurance and confidence.
- **Intermediate Runners:** Increase mileage progressively while incorporating quality workouts (tempo runs, intervals) to improve fitness and race performance.
- **Advanced Runners:** Fine-tune training volume and intensity based on race goals, focusing on specificity and performance optimization.

Monitoring Mileage and Listen to Your Body

- **Training Logs:** Keep a detailed training log to track mileage, workout intensity, perceived effort, and recovery indicators.
- **Physical Signals:** Listen to your body's feedback, including fatigue, soreness, and changes in performance, to adjust training volume and intensity as needed.
- **Consulting Professionals:** Seek guidance from experienced coaches,

physical therapists, or healthcare professionals to address training-related concerns and optimize performance safely.

Cross-Training and Strength Training

Cross-training and strength training complement running by enhancing muscular balance, reducing injury risk, and improving overall fitness. This section explores the benefits of incorporating diverse training modalities into your marathon preparation.

Benefits of Cross-Training

- **Muscular Balance:** Engages different muscle groups and movement patterns, preventing overuse injuries common in repetitive running.
- **Cardiovascular Fitness:** Improves aerobic capacity without the impact stress of running, promoting recovery and enhancing overall endurance.
- **Mental Refreshment:** Provides variety and enjoyment in training, reducing monotony and burnout associated with long-distance running.

Types of Cross-Training

- **Cycling:** Low-impact activity that improves cardiovascular fitness and leg strength while providing active recovery between running sessions.

- **Swimming:** Full-body workout that enhances aerobic endurance, muscular strength, and flexibility without joint stress.
- **Elliptical or Rowing:** Mimics running motion while reducing impact on joints, promoting aerobic conditioning and lower-body strength development.
- **Yoga or Pilates:** Enhances flexibility, core strength, and body awareness, improving running posture and injury prevention.

Integrating Cross-Training into Marathon Training

- **Weekly Schedule:** Schedule cross-training sessions on non-running days or as active recovery between hard workouts to maintain fitness and promote recovery.
- **Intensity and Duration:** Match cross-training intensity (low to moderate) and duration (30-60 minutes) to complement running workouts without compromising recovery or causing undue fatigue.
- **Progression and Adaptation:** Gradually increase cross-training volume and intensity as fitness improves, focusing on specific goals (endurance, strength, flexibility) relevant to marathon performance.

Takeaway

Building your base is the foundational phase of marathon training, focusing on developing aerobic endurance, gradually increasing mileage, and incorporating cross-training and strength training to support overall fitness and injury prevention. By understanding the principles of endurance training, progressing mileage safely, and diversifying your training regimen, you lay a solid foundation for long-term success in marathon preparation.

In the chapters that follow, we will delve deeper into practical strategies for nutrition and hydration, injury prevention techniques, mental preparation strategies, race day preparations, and post-marathon recovery. By integrating these elements into your training program, you will enhance your readiness, optimize performance, and embrace the challenges and rewards of completing a marathon.

Chapter 4: Nutrition and Hydration

Nutrition and hydration play pivotal roles in marathon training and race day success. This chapter explores the fundamentals of fueling strategies, hydration principles, and post-run recovery nutrition to optimize performance, support endurance, and promote overall well-being throughout your marathon journey.

Fueling Your Runs

Proper nutrition before, during, and after training runs is essential for sustaining energy levels, enhancing performance, and supporting recovery. This section delves into strategies for pre-run fueling, during-run nutrition, and post-run recovery to meet the demands of marathon training.

Pre-Run Nutrition Strategies

Fueling your body adequately before training runs and long-distance efforts ensures optimal energy levels and performance. Key considerations include:

- **Carbohydrates:** Consuming complex carbohydrates (whole grains, fruits, vegetables) to provide sustained energy and replenish glycogen stores.
- **Proteins:** Including lean proteins (chicken, fish, legumes) to support muscle repair and recovery.
- **Fats:** Incorporating healthy fats (avocado, nuts, seeds) for sustained energy and satiety during longer runs.
- **Timing:** Eating a balanced meal or snack containing carbohydrates and proteins 2-3 hours before a run to allow for digestion and nutrient absorption.

Pre-Run Meal and Snack Ideas

- **Morning Runs:** Oatmeal with fruit and nuts, whole-grain toast with nut butter, or yogurt with granola and berries.

- **Afternoon/Evening Runs:** Whole-grain pasta with lean protein (chicken, tofu), quinoa salad with vegetables and chickpeas, or a smoothie with banana, spinach, and protein powder.

During-Run Fueling Options

Maintaining energy levels and hydration during long runs is crucial for sustained performance. Strategies for during-run nutrition include:

- **Energy Gels:** Quick-digesting carbohydrates in gel form to provide immediate energy and electrolytes.
- **Sports Drinks:** Fluids containing carbohydrates and electrolytes (sodium, potassium) to replenish electrolyte losses and maintain hydration.
- **Whole Foods:** Portable options such as bananas, energy bars, or pretzels for carbohydrate and electrolyte replenishment during extended efforts.

Tailoring Fueling Strategies

- **Individual Preferences:** Experiment with different types and flavors of energy gels, sports drinks, and whole foods to identify what works best for your stomach and energy needs during training.

- **Practice Runs:** Simulate race-day conditions by testing fueling strategies during long training runs to refine timing, quantities, and combinations for optimal performance.

Hydration Basics

Maintaining proper hydration is critical for regulating body temperature, supporting cardiovascular function, and maximizing exercise performance. This section explores hydration principles, fluid requirements, and strategies for optimizing hydration status during marathon training.

Importance of Hydration

Hydration impacts overall health, exercise performance, and recovery. Benefits of proper hydration include:

- **Temperature Regulation:** Sweating helps dissipate heat and maintain core body temperature during physical exertion.
- **Cardiovascular Function:** Adequate hydration supports blood circulation and oxygen delivery to working muscles.
- **Performance Optimization:** Maintaining fluid balance enhances endurance, muscular strength, and cognitive function during prolonged exercise.

Calculating Fluid Needs

Individual fluid requirements vary based on factors such as sweat rate, environmental conditions, and exercise intensity. Strategies for calculating fluid needs include:

- **Sweat Rate Measurement:** Weighing yourself before and after a training run to estimate fluid losses (1 pound of weight loss = approximately 16 ounces of fluid deficit).
- **Hydration Guidelines:** Aim to consume 16-24 ounces of fluid per pound of body weight lost during exercise to replenish fluid losses and maintain hydration status.
- **Thirst Sensation:** Drink according to thirst cues during training runs to prevent dehydration without overhydrating.

Electrolyte Replacement

Electrolytes (sodium, potassium, magnesium) play crucial roles in fluid balance, muscle contraction, and nerve function. Strategies for electrolyte replacement include:

- **Sports Drinks:** Choose electrolyte-rich sports drinks or electrolyte tablets to replenish sodium and potassium lost through sweat.

- **Whole Foods:** Include potassium-rich foods (bananas, oranges, potatoes) and magnesium sources (nuts, seeds, leafy greens) in your diet to support electrolyte balance.
- **Supplements:** Consider electrolyte supplements or salt tablets during prolonged training sessions or races in hot, humid conditions.

Pre- and Post-Run Nutrition

Optimizing pre- and post-run nutrition supports energy production, muscle repair, and recovery. This section provides strategies for timing meals and snacks around training sessions and maximizing nutrient intake to enhance marathon training outcomes.

Timing Meals and Snacks

- **Pre-Run:** Eat a balanced meal containing carbohydrates and proteins 2-3 hours before a training run to provide sustained energy and support muscle function.
- **Post-Run:** Consume a recovery meal or snack containing carbohydrates and proteins within 30-60 minutes after a run to replenish glycogen stores and promote muscle repair.

Recovery Nutrition Strategies

- **Carbohydrates:** Replenish glycogen stores with high-carbohydrate foods such as whole grains, fruits, and starchy vegetables.
- **Proteins:** Support muscle repair and recovery with lean proteins (chicken, fish, tofu), dairy products, or plant-based protein sources (beans, lentils).
- **Hydration:** Rehydrate with fluids containing electrolytes (sports drinks, water with electrolyte tablets) to replace fluid losses and support recovery.

Nutritional Considerations for Race Day

Preparing for race day involves fine-tuning nutrition strategies to optimize energy levels, hydration status, and gastrointestinal comfort. Key considerations include:

- **Race Week Nutrition:** Gradually increase carbohydrate intake leading up to race day to maximize glycogen stores and minimize gastrointestinal distress.
- **Pre-Race Meal:** Eat a familiar, easily digestible meal containing carbohydrates and proteins 2-3 hours before the race start to fuel performance without causing stomach upset.
- **During-Race Fueling Plan:** Implement a structured fueling plan incorporating energy gels, sports

drinks, and whole foods to maintain
energy levels and hydration
throughout the marathon distance.

Takeaway

Nutrition and hydration are integral
components of marathon training, influencing
performance, recovery, and overall well-being.
By understanding the principles of fueling
strategies, hydration requirements, and post-
run nutrition, you can optimize training
adaptations, support endurance development,
and prepare effectively for race day challenges.

In the chapters that follow, we will delve
deeper into practical strategies for injury
prevention, mental preparation techniques,
race day preparations, and post-marathon
recovery. By integrating comprehensive
nutrition and hydration practices into your
marathon training program, you will enhance
your readiness, optimize performance, and
achieve your marathon goals with confidence.

Chapter 5: Injury Prevention

Injury prevention is crucial for maintaining consistency in marathon training and achieving peak performance on race day. This chapter explores common running injuries, proactive strategies for injury prevention, and effective recovery techniques to support your marathon journey.

Common Running Injuries and How to Avoid Them

Running imposes repetitive stress on the body, making runners susceptible to various injuries.

Understanding the causes, symptoms, and preventive measures for common running injuries is essential for minimizing setbacks and optimizing training progression.

1. Runner's Knee (Patellofemoral Pain Syndrome)

- **Causes:** Overuse, improper running mechanics (e.g., overpronation), muscular imbalances (weak hips or quads), and inadequate footwear.
- **Symptoms:** Dull, aching pain around the kneecap, aggravated by running, going up or down stairs, or prolonged sitting.
- **Prevention:** Strengthen quadriceps, hips, and core muscles; improve running form; wear proper shoes; and gradually increase mileage.

2. IT Band Syndrome

- **Causes:** Tightness or inflammation of the iliotibial (IT) band due to repetitive friction over the knee joint.
- **Symptoms:** Sharp or burning pain on the outside of the knee, aggravated by running downhill or prolonged periods of running.
- **Prevention:** Stretch IT band and surrounding muscles (hip flexors, glutes), incorporate foam rolling, avoid excessive downhill running, and maintain proper running shoes.

3. Shin Splints (Medial Tibial Stress Syndrome)

- **Causes:** Overuse, sudden increases in mileage or intensity, running on hard surfaces, and biomechanical factors (overpronation).
- **Symptoms:** Pain along the inner edge of the shinbone (tibia), especially during or after running.
- **Prevention:** Gradually increase mileage, incorporate cross-training (cycling, swimming), strengthen calf and shin muscles, use proper footwear, and ensure adequate recovery.

4. Achilles Tendinitis

- **Causes:** Overuse, sudden changes in training intensity, tight calf muscles, improper footwear, and running on uneven surfaces.
- **Symptoms:** Pain and stiffness in the Achilles tendon area, particularly during the initial steps of a run or after prolonged rest.
- **Prevention:** Stretch and strengthen calf muscles, avoid sudden increases in mileage, incorporate rest and recovery days, and use appropriate footwear with adequate support.

5. Plantar Fasciitis

- **Causes:** Inflammation of the plantar fascia due to overuse, tight calf muscles, improper footwear, or sudden changes in training.

- **Symptoms:** Pain and stiffness in the heel or arch of the foot, particularly in the morning or after prolonged sitting.
- **Prevention:** Stretch calf and foot muscles, wear supportive shoes with arch support, avoid running on hard surfaces, and use orthotic inserts if necessary.

6. Stress Fractures

- **Causes:** Overuse, repetitive stress, inadequate recovery, nutritional deficiencies (calcium, vitamin D), and biomechanical factors.
- **Symptoms:** Localized pain, swelling, and tenderness over the affected bone, exacerbated by weight-bearing activities.
- **Prevention:** Gradually increase mileage, incorporate cross-training, ensure proper nutrition and adequate rest, and seek prompt medical evaluation for persistent pain or symptoms.

Strategies for Injury Prevention

Proactive measures can significantly reduce the risk of running injuries and maintain consistency in marathon training. Implementing a comprehensive injury prevention plan involves addressing biomechanical factors, improving running mechanics, and integrating strength and flexibility exercises into your training regimen.

1. Biomechanical Assessment

- **Gait Analysis:** Consult with a running coach or physical therapist for a gait analysis to identify biomechanical issues (e.g., overpronation, supination) that contribute to injury risk.
- **Footwear Evaluation:** Choose running shoes appropriate for your foot type and running mechanics to provide adequate support, cushioning, and stability.

2. Running Form and Technique

- **Stride Length and Cadence:** Focus on maintaining a moderate stride length and increasing cadence (steps per minute) to reduce impact forces and improve running efficiency.
- **Posture and Alignment:** Maintain proper posture (head over shoulders, shoulders over hips) and alignment (knees tracking over feet) to minimize stress on joints and muscles.

3. Strength Training for Runners

- **Core Strength:** Perform exercises to strengthen core muscles (abdominals, obliques, lower back) to stabilize the spine and pelvis during running.

- **Lower Body Strength:** Incorporate exercises targeting leg muscles (quadriceps, hamstrings, calves) to improve muscular endurance and support proper running mechanics.
- **Hip and Glute Activation:** Activate and strengthen hip abductors (gluteus medius), adductors, and external rotators to improve hip stability and reduce risk of IT band syndrome and knee injuries.

4. Flexibility and Mobility

- **Dynamic Warm-Up:** Perform dynamic stretches and mobility drills before running to increase blood flow, improve range of motion, and prepare muscles for activity.
- **Static Stretching:** Incorporate static stretches (held for 15-30 seconds) after running to improve flexibility, reduce muscle tension, and enhance recovery.

5. Gradual Progression and Recovery

- **Training Volume:** Gradually increase mileage and intensity to allow for adaptation and recovery between training sessions.
- **Rest and Active Recovery:** Incorporate rest days and

active recovery activities (swimming, cycling, yoga) to promote tissue repair, glycogen replenishment, and mental rejuvenation.
- **Listen to Your Body:** Pay attention to early signs of fatigue, discomfort, or changes in performance, and adjust training accordingly to prevent overuse injuries.

Effective Recovery Techniques

Recovery is integral to injury prevention and performance optimization during marathon training. Implementing effective recovery strategies enhances muscle repair, reduces inflammation, and promotes overall well-being.

1. Nutrition for Recovery

- **Carbohydrates:** Replenish glycogen stores with high-carbohydrate foods (whole grains, fruits, vegetables) to support energy restoration and muscle recovery.
- **Proteins:** Consume lean proteins (chicken, fish, beans) to promote muscle repair and synthesis after strenuous workouts.
- **Hydration:** Drink fluids containing electrolytes (sports drinks, water with electrolyte tablets) to replace fluid losses and support hydration status.

2. Compression Therapy

- **Compression Garments:** Wear compression socks, sleeves, or tights to improve circulation, reduce muscle soreness, and expedite recovery.
- **Compression Boots:** Use pneumatic compression devices to enhance venous return, reduce swelling, and facilitate muscle recovery after long runs or intense training sessions.

3. Foam Rolling and Self-Myofascial Release

- **Foam Roller:** Perform self-myofascial release techniques using a foam roller to alleviate muscle tightness, improve flexibility, and enhance recovery between workouts.
- **Trigger Point Therapy:** Target specific areas of muscle tension or trigger points with a foam roller, massage ball, or handheld massage tool to release knots and improve muscle function.

4. Ice Baths and Contrast Therapy

- **Ice Baths:** Submerge legs and lower body in cold water (50-59°F or 10-15°C) for 10-15 minutes to reduce inflammation, numb pain, and accelerate muscle recovery.
- **Contrast Therapy:** Alternate between hot (90-105°F or 32-40°C) and cold water immersion to improve circulation, reduce muscle soreness,

and promote recovery after intense training.

Takeaway

Injury prevention is essential for maintaining consistency, optimizing performance, and achieving marathon training goals. By understanding common running injuries, implementing proactive prevention strategies, and integrating effective recovery techniques, you can minimize setbacks, enhance training adaptation, and prepare effectively for the physical demands of marathon running.

In the chapters that follow, we will delve deeper into practical strategies for mental preparation techniques, race day preparations, and post-marathon recovery. By prioritizing injury prevention and recovery as integral components of your marathon training program, you will build resilience, improve performance outcomes, and embrace the challenges and rewards of completing a marathon with confidence.

Chapter 6: Mental Preparation

Mental preparation is as vital as physical training in marathon preparation. This chapter explores strategies to develop mental toughness, manage pre-race nerves, harness visualization techniques, set effective goals, and maintain motivation to achieve peak performance on race day.

Overcoming Mental Barriers

Running a marathon challenges both the body and mind. Overcoming mental barriers involves understanding common challenges, developing coping strategies, and cultivating resilience to navigate obstacles encountered during training and on race day.

Understanding Mental Barriers

- **Pre-Race Nerves:** Anxiety and self-doubt before a race can impact performance and confidence.
- **Physical Discomfort:** Managing fatigue, discomfort, and pain during long-distance efforts.
- **Negative Self-Talk:** Overcoming inner critic and maintaining positive mindset.
- **Fear of Failure:** Coping with fear of not achieving goals or meeting expectations.

Coping Strategies

- **Mindfulness and Relaxation Techniques:** Practice deep breathing, progressive muscle relaxation, or meditation to calm nerves and reduce anxiety.
- **Positive Self-Talk:** Replace negative thoughts with affirmations and encouragement to build confidence and maintain focus.
- **Focus on Process:** Emphasize effort, strategy, and execution rather than solely focusing on outcomes.

- **Visualize Success:** Visualize successful training runs and race day scenarios to reinforce belief in capabilities and goals.

Developing Mental Toughness

- **Resilience:** Embrace challenges, setbacks, and adversity as opportunities for growth and learning.
- **Adaptability:** Adjust to unexpected circumstances, weather conditions, and race day challenges with flexibility and composure.
- **Grit and Determination:** Maintain persistence, motivation, and commitment to long-term goals despite obstacles or setbacks.

Visualization and Goal Setting

Visualization and goal setting are powerful tools for enhancing performance, maintaining motivation, and achieving success in marathon training. This section explores techniques to visualize success, set SMART goals, and track progress throughout your training journey.

Visualization Techniques

- **Imagery:** Create vivid mental images of successful training runs, crossing the finish line, and overcoming challenges.

- **Multi-Sensory Visualization:** Engage all senses (sight, sound, touch, smell, taste) to immerse yourself in positive race day experiences.
- **Race Day Scenarios:** Visualize race day logistics, pacing strategies, and overcoming obstacles with confidence and determination.

Benefits of Visualization

- **Performance Enhancement:** Enhance confidence, mental rehearsal, and preparation for race day challenges.
- **Stress Reduction:** Manage pre-race nerves, anxiety, and uncertainty through mental preparation and visualization techniques.
- **Goal Alignment:** Align mental imagery with specific race goals, performance objectives, and desired outcomes.

Setting Effective Goals

- **SMART Goals:** Specific, Measurable, Achievable, Relevant, Time-bound goals that provide clarity, direction, and accountability in marathon training.
- **Process-Oriented Goals:** Focus on training consistency, incremental

improvements, and mastering race day strategies.

- **Outcome-Oriented Goals:** Define desired race results, personal bests, and performance benchmarks to strive towards during training.

- **Training Logs:** Maintain a detailed training log to monitor mileage, workout intensity, recovery metrics, and emotional well-being.
- **Performance Metrics:** Track race times, splits, personal bests, and milestones achieved throughout marathon training.
- **Self-Assessment:** Reflect on progress, setbacks, and adjustments made to training plans to inform future goals and training strategies.

Staying Motivated

Maintaining motivation throughout marathon training involves establishing routines, cultivating support networks, embracing variety, and celebrating milestones to sustain enthusiasm and commitment towards achieving your marathon goals.

Establishing Support Networks

- **Training Partners:** Join running clubs, training groups, or virtual communities to share experiences, encouragement, and accountability.

- **Coaching and Mentorship:** Seek guidance from experienced coaches, mentors, or advisors to provide expert advice, feedback, and support.
- **Family and Friends:** Share training progress, challenges, and achievements with loved ones for encouragement and motivation.

Incorporating Variety

- **Training Diversity:** Mix up training routines with cross-training activities (cycling, swimming, yoga) to prevent monotony and enhance overall fitness.
- **Terrain and Routes:** Explore different running routes, trails, or scenic locations to maintain interest, motivation, and enjoyment in training.
- **Workout Challenges:** Set personal challenges, such as speed workouts, hill repeats, or distance milestones, to foster improvement and excitement in training.

Celebrating Milestones

- **Progress Recognition:** Acknowledge and celebrate incremental improvements, personal bests, and training milestones achieved throughout marathon preparation.

- **Reward System:** Establish rewards (e.g., new running gear, massage, leisure activities) for achieving training goals and maintaining consistency in training.

Takeaway

Mental preparation is essential for building resilience, maintaining motivation, and optimizing performance in marathon training. By overcoming mental barriers, harnessing visualization techniques, setting effective goals, and staying motivated throughout your training journey, you can cultivate the mental toughness and confidence needed to achieve your marathon goals with determination and success.

In the chapters that follow, we will delve deeper into practical strategies for race day preparations, recovery techniques, and post-marathon reflections. By prioritizing mental preparation as a fundamental component of marathon training, you will enhance your readiness, resilience, and enjoyment in pursuing and completing a marathon with confidence and fulfillment.

Chapter 7: Long Runs and Race Preparation

Increasing Mileage Safely

Long runs are the cornerstone of marathon training, essential for building endurance, mental toughness, and race day readiness. Safely increasing mileage over the course of your training cycle is crucial to prevent injury, promote adaptation, and prepare your body for the demands of marathon distance.

Establishing a Base

Begin your marathon training with a base mileage that aligns with your current fitness level and running experience. This foundation sets the stage for progressive mileage increases throughout your training cycle:

- **Assessing Current Fitness:** Evaluate your current running mileage and endurance capabilities to establish a baseline for initiating marathon training.
- **Gradual Progression:** Increase weekly mileage incrementally (10-20% per week) to allow for adaptation, minimize injury risk, and promote sustainable growth in endurance.
- **Monitoring Recovery:** Pay attention to signs of fatigue, soreness, or overtraining, adjusting mileage and intensity as needed to prioritize recovery and long-term progress.

Progressive Build-Up

Progressively increase long run distance to simulate and surpass marathon distance, gradually conditioning your body to sustain prolonged effort:

- **Long Run Progression:** Start with shorter long runs (e.g., 10-12 miles) and gradually extend distance over successive weeks to peak long runs (e.g., 20-22 miles) in the final phase of training.

- **Incremental Increases:** Incorporate step-back weeks with reduced mileage or intensity to facilitate recovery and prevent cumulative fatigue.
- **Weekly Mileage Goals:** Aim for weekly mileage goals that align with your training plan and race day objectives, balancing long runs with shorter, recovery-focused runs throughout the week.

Cross-Training and Recovery

Integrate cross-training activities such as swimming, cycling, or yoga to complement running, improve overall fitness, and enhance recovery between long runs:

- **Low-Impact Alternatives:** Engage in low-impact cross-training activities on non-running days to maintain aerobic fitness, strengthen supporting muscles, and reduce injury risk.
- **Active Recovery:** Incorporate active recovery techniques such as foam rolling, stretching, and massage to promote muscle recovery, alleviate tightness, and enhance mobility.
- **Rest and Regeneration:** Prioritize rest days to allow for complete physical and mental recovery, recognizing the importance of sleep, hydration, and nutrition in supporting marathon training demands.

Simulating Race Day Conditions

Effective race preparation involves simulating race day conditions during long runs to familiarize yourself with marathon-specific challenges, refine strategies, and build confidence in your ability to perform on race day.

Environmental Factors

Consider environmental variables such as weather conditions, terrain, and course elevation when planning long runs to replicate race day scenarios:

- **Weather Adaptation:** Train in varying weather conditions (e.g., heat, humidity, wind) to acclimate your body, practice hydration strategies, and adjust pacing accordingly.
- **Terrain Variation:** Incorporate long runs on diverse terrain (e.g., hills, flats) to simulate race course challenges, refine technique, and adapt pacing strategies to specific course profiles.
- **Altitude Training:** If relevant to your race, incorporate altitude training or simulate elevation changes during long runs to enhance aerobic capacity and respiratory efficiency.

Nutrition and Hydration Practices

Practice race day nutrition and hydration strategies during long runs to optimize fueling, maintain energy levels, and prevent gastrointestinal issues:

- **Pre-Race Nutrition:** Experiment with pre-run meals and timing to identify foods that provide sustained energy without digestive discomfort during long runs and race day.
- **During-Run Fueling:** Test energy gels, sports drinks, or whole foods for fueling intervals and quantities that meet your energy needs and support endurance performance.
- **Hydration Management:** Practice drinking water or electrolyte beverages at planned intervals to maintain hydration status, replace electrolytes lost through sweat, and prevent dehydration during extended efforts.

Gear and Equipment Testing

Use long runs as opportunities to test and adjust race day gear, including shoes, apparel, hydration systems, and nutrition accessories:

- **Shoe Selection:** Choose running shoes that provide comfort, support, and durability over long distances, testing different models and ensuring proper fit to minimize risk of blisters or discomfort.

- **Apparel Considerations:** Select moisture-wicking, breathable clothing suitable for race day conditions, including layers for temperature regulation and protection from sun or inclement weather.
- **Hydration Strategies:** Experiment with hydration belts, handheld bottles, or vest systems during long runs to determine the most comfortable and efficient setup for carrying fluids and electrolytes.

Pacing Strategies

Mastering pacing strategies during long runs is essential for optimizing race day performance, managing effort, and achieving consistent splits throughout the marathon distance:

Goal Setting and Race Planning

Set realistic pacing goals based on training progress, fitness assessments, and race day objectives to guide long run execution and overall race strategy:

- **Target Race Pace:** Identify target marathon pace (e.g., minutes per mile or kilometers) based on fitness assessments, recent race performances, and training outcomes.
- **Segmented Pacing Strategy:** Divide the marathon distance into manageable segments or splits,

establishing pace zones for different phases of the race to conserve energy and maintain race day strategy.

Long Run Execution

Implement pacing strategies during long runs to practice race day scenarios, refine split management, and build confidence in pacing discipline:

- **Conservative Start:** Begin long runs at a comfortable, sustainable pace slightly slower than goal marathon pace to conserve energy, assess physical readiness, and practice negative splits.
- **Progressive Build-Up:** Gradually increase pace or effort throughout the long run to simulate fatigue resistance, test pacing strategies, and practice finishing strong over extended distances.

Mental Focus and Resilience

Develop mental strategies during long runs to enhance focus, resilience, and positive mindset throughout the marathon distance:

- **Mental Toughness:** Embrace challenges, setbacks, and discomfort during long runs as opportunities to strengthen mental resilience, practice coping strategies, and cultivate race day determination.

- **Visualization and Mantras:** Use visualization techniques and personalized mantras to reinforce positive mindset, maintain motivation, and stay focused on performance goals during long runs and race day.

Takeaway

Long runs are fundamental to marathon training, providing opportunities to increase mileage safely, simulate race day conditions, and master pacing strategies essential for achieving race day success. By integrating structured long runs into your training regimen, refining race preparation techniques, and honing pacing skills, you can optimize marathon performance and achieve personal milestones with confidence, determination, and resilience.

In the upcoming chapters, we will explore tapering strategies, final race day preparations, and post-marathon recovery techniques to support your marathon journey from start to finish. By embracing the holistic approach to marathon training, you will continue to evolve as a marathoner, setting new goals, and inspiring others through your dedication to endurance, resilience, and the pursuit of excellence.

Chapter 8: Tapering and Final Preparations

Understanding Tapering

Tapering is a deliberate reduction in training volume and intensity in the weeks leading up to a marathon. This phase allows your body to recover from the rigors of training, maximize muscle glycogen stores, repair any micro-damage to muscles, and ensure you approach race day feeling fresh, fit, and mentally prepared.

The Science Behind Tapering

Tapering is grounded in exercise physiology principles, aiming to balance fitness retention with recovery. During tapering:

- **Muscle Repair and Adaptation:** Reduced training load allows muscles to repair and adapt to the stress imposed during training, minimizing the risk of injury and enhancing overall readiness.
- **Glycogen Replenishment:** Tapering increases muscle glycogen stores, optimizing energy availability for sustained endurance performance on race day.
- **Neuromuscular Adaptations:** Rest and reduced training intensity improve neuromuscular coordination, enhancing muscular efficiency and stride economy.

Tapering Period and Duration

Tapering typically begins 2-3 weeks before race day, with the duration varying based on individual fitness level, training history, and race distance. Key aspects of tapering include:

- **Progressive Reduction:** Gradually decrease training volume and intensity over the tapering period while maintaining some level of intensity to preserve fitness gains.
- **Peak Week:** The final week before the marathon involves significant

reduction in mileage and intensity to allow for complete recovery and optimal race day readiness.

- **Tapering Milestones:** Monitor your body's response to tapering, adjusting based on feedback to strike a balance between rest and maintaining race day fitness.

Managing Tapering Challenges

Tapering can evoke mixed emotions, including restlessness, uncertainty, and heightened awareness of physical sensations. Strategies to manage tapering challenges include:

- **Trust in Training:** Reflect on your training progression, acknowledging the hard work and dedication that have prepared you for race day.
- **Stay Active:** Engage in light activities such as easy runs, yoga, or mobility exercises to maintain physical and mental well-being during tapering.
- **Nutrition and Hydration:** Pay attention to balanced nutrition and hydration to support recovery and optimize energy levels for race day performance.
- **Mindfulness and Relaxation:** Practice relaxation techniques, such as deep breathing, meditation, or visualization, to alleviate pre-race nerves and foster mental clarity.

Fine-Tuning Your Race Day Plan

Fine-tuning your race day plan involves refining pacing strategies, nutrition protocols, gear choices, and logistical details to align with your race day goals and maximize performance potential.

Pacing Strategy Refinement

Based on your training and tapering experiences, adjust your race day pacing strategy to optimize performance while accounting for course terrain, weather conditions, and personal fitness level:

- **Race Pace Goals:** Set realistic pace goals aligned with your training outcomes and race day objectives (e.g., finishing time, personal best).
- **Segmented Approach:** Break down the marathon distance into manageable segments, focusing on pacing consistency and strategic effort distribution throughout the race.
- **Adaptability:** Be prepared to adjust pacing based on real-time feedback, environmental factors, and internal cues to maintain optimal performance and energy preservation.

Nutrition and Hydration Protocols

Review and practice your race day nutrition and hydration plan during the tapering phase to fine-tune fueling strategies, optimize energy intake, and minimize gastrointestinal distress:

- **Pre-Race Nutrition:** Continue carbohydrate loading in the days leading up to the marathon, focusing on easily digestible meals that support glycogen replenishment and hydration.
- **Race Morning Fuel:** Plan a balanced pre-race breakfast rich in carbohydrates and moderate in protein and fats, tailored to your digestive tolerance and energy needs.
- **During-Race Fueling:** Experiment with energy gels, sports drinks, and hydration strategies during final long runs to identify optimal fueling intervals, amounts, and hydration needs based on anticipated race day conditions.

Gear and Equipment Preparation

Ensure all race day gear, including shoes, apparel, hydration systems, and accessories, is thoroughly tested and prepared to enhance comfort, performance, and logistical efficiency:

- **Shoe Selection:** Choose well-worn, supportive running shoes that provide comfort and stability over marathon distances, avoiding last-minute changes to minimize risk of blisters or discomfort.

- **Clothing and Weather Readiness:** Check weather forecasts to select appropriate attire that balances comfort, moisture management, and protection from sun or rain during the race.
- **Race Day Essentials:** Pack a race day bag containing bib number, timing chip, nutrition supplies, sunscreen, and any personal items needed for pre- and post-race comfort and convenience.

Logistics and Race Day Preparation

Plan logistical details such as transportation, accommodation, race day schedule, and support crew arrangements to minimize stress and ensure a smooth transition from pre-race preparation to race day execution:

- **Travel Arrangements:** Confirm travel plans, accommodation reservations, and transportation logistics to arrive at the race venue with ample time for registration, gear check, and pre-race rituals.
- **Race Packet Pickup:** Collect bib number, timing chip, and race day information in advance to avoid last-minute rushes and familiarize yourself with race day procedures and course details.
- **Pre-Race Routine:** Establish a pre-race routine that includes warm-up

exercises, mental preparation techniques, and final gear checks to optimize readiness and focus before the starting line.

Mental Preparation in the Final Week

The final week before the marathon is a period of mental sharpening, confidence-building, and emotional readiness. Harnessing mental preparation techniques ensures you approach race day with a positive mindset, resilience, and mental clarity.

Visualize Race Day Success

Visualize yourself crossing the finish line strong, achieving race day goals, and overcoming challenges with determination and composure:

- **Visualization Practice:** Dedicate time each day to visualize race scenarios, envisioning positive outcomes, overcoming obstacles, and maintaining focus on performance goals.
- **Embrace Confidence:** Reflect on your training achievements, strengths, and preparation efforts to reinforce self-belief and confidence in your ability to perform on race day.

Manage Pre-Race Nerves

Acknowledge and manage pre-race nerves through mindfulness, relaxation techniques, and proactive mental preparation strategies:

- **Deep Breathing:** Incorporate deep breathing exercises to calm nerves, regulate heart rate, and enhance mental focus during moments of pre-race anticipation.
- **Positive Self-Talk:** Replace doubts or negative thoughts with positive affirmations, focusing on your readiness, training accomplishments, and excitement for the upcoming challenge.

Mental Rehearsal and Strategy

Review and rehearse your race day strategy, including pacing, fueling, hydration, and race course familiarity, to enhance mental readiness and tactical decision-making:

- **Race Plan Review:** Review your race day plan, considering potential scenarios, race-specific adjustments, and contingency strategies to adapt to changing conditions or challenges.
- **Mindful Awareness:** Stay present in the moment, focusing on each phase of race day execution with mindfulness, awareness of physical sensations, and appreciation for the marathon journey.

Takeaway

Tapering and final preparations are pivotal phases in marathon training, culminating in race day readiness, physical peak performance, and mental resilience. By understanding the science of tapering, fine-tuning your race day plan, and embracing mental preparation techniques, you can optimize your marathon experience and achieve your race day goals with confidence, determination, and enjoyment.

In the chapters ahead, we will explore post-marathon recovery strategies, injury prevention techniques, and reflections on the transformative impact of marathon training. By integrating comprehensive tapering and final preparation strategies into your marathon journey, you will cultivate endurance, resilience, and fulfillment in pursuing and completing marathons with passion and dedication.

Chapter 9: Race Day

Morning Routine and Breakfast

Race day begins long before the starting gun fires, with careful attention to morning routines and breakfast choices essential for setting the stage for optimal performance and comfort throughout the marathon.

Pre-Race Morning Routine

Establishing a structured pre-race morning routine helps streamline preparations, minimize stress, and mentally prepare for the challenges ahead:

- **Early Wake-Up:** Rise early to allow ample time for pre-race rituals, breakfast consumption, and travel to the race venue without rushing.
- **Hydration Protocol:** Begin hydrating immediately upon waking to optimize fluid balance and support muscle function throughout the marathon.
- **Light Stretching:** Engage in gentle stretching or mobility exercises to promote blood flow, alleviate pre-race jitters, and prepare muscles for physical exertion.

Breakfast Choices for Marathoners

Choosing the right pre-race breakfast is crucial for sustaining energy levels, optimizing glycogen stores, and minimizing gastrointestinal discomfort during the marathon:

- **Carbohydrate-Rich Options:** Select high-carbohydrate, moderate-protein, and low-fat foods such as oatmeal, whole-grain toast with banana, or energy bars to fuel prolonged endurance efforts.
- **Digestive Tolerance:** Stick to familiar foods that are easily digestible and well-tolerated to avoid unexpected gastrointestinal issues on race day.
- **Timing:** Consume breakfast 2-3 hours before the race start to allow for

digestion and nutrient absorption, adjusting timing based on personal preferences and digestive comfort.

Hydration Strategy

Hydrate strategically in the hours leading up to the marathon to maintain optimal fluid balance, support thermoregulation, and prevent dehydration during exertion:

- **Pre-Race Hydration:** Drink water or electrolyte beverages consistently in the hours before the race, monitoring urine color and fluid intake to ensure hydration adequacy.
- **Avoid Overhydration:** Balance hydration efforts to prevent overconsumption, which can lead to hyponatremia or discomfort during the marathon.
- **Electrolyte Considerations:** Include electrolyte-rich beverages or supplements to replenish sodium and potassium lost through sweat, especially in warmer climates or longer race durations.

Warm-Up Exercises

Effective warm-up exercises prime your muscles, enhance neuromuscular coordination, and mentally prepare for the demands of marathon running, ensuring a smooth

transition from pre-race routines to the starting
line:

Dynamic Warm-Up Routine

Engage in a dynamic warm-up routine tailored
to activate major muscle groups, improve
range of motion, and elevate heart rate
gradually before the marathon:

- **Joint Mobilization:** Perform gentle
  joint rotations and movements to
  increase flexibility, reduce stiffness,
  and promote optimal joint function
  during running.
- **Dynamic Stretching:** Incorporate
  dynamic stretches such as leg swings,
  walking lunges, and high knees to
  activate muscles, stimulate blood flow,
  and prepare for running mechanics.
- **Strides or Accelerations:** Include
  short bursts of running at race pace or
  faster to simulate race conditions,
  activate fast-twitch muscle fibers, and
  mentally rehearse stride mechanics.

Mental Preparation

Use the warm-up period as an opportunity to
focus mentally, visualize race day success, and
cultivate a positive mindset before lining up at
the starting line:

- **Visual Imagery:** Picture yourself
  executing race strategies, overcoming

challenges, and achieving performance goals with confidence and determination.

- **Affirmations and Mantras:** Repeat positive affirmations or personalized mantras to reinforce mental toughness, boost self-belief, and stay focused on the present moment.
- **Deep Breathing:** Incorporate deep breathing exercises to calm nerves, regulate breathing patterns, and promote relaxation amidst pre-race excitement.

Strategies for Race Day Success

Executing a well-crafted race day strategy involves pacing discipline, fueling consistency, mental resilience, and adaptability to race day conditions. Here's how to navigate the marathon distance with confidence and achieve your performance goals:

Starting Line Preparation

Position yourself strategically at the starting line based on anticipated pace goals, race objectives, and personal preferences for navigating initial race congestion:

- **Corral Placement:** Select an appropriate corral or starting wave aligned with your projected finish time, allowing for clear passage and minimizing early race congestion.

- **Visual Cues:** Identify landmarks or pacers within your target pace group to maintain pacing discipline and monitor progress throughout the marathon.

Implement a well-calibrated pacing strategy to conserve energy, manage fatigue, and maintain sustainable effort across the marathon distance:

- **Conservative Start:** Begin the marathon at a slightly slower pace than goal race pace to conserve glycogen stores, acclimate to race conditions, and avoid early fatigue.
- **Negative Splits:** Aim for negative splits by gradually increasing pace in the second half of the marathon, leveraging accumulated energy reserves and mental resilience for strong finish.

Execute your race day nutrition and hydration plan meticulously, leveraging pre-race experimentation and hydration stations to sustain energy levels and optimize performance:

- **Fueling Intervals:** Consume energy gels, sports drinks, or snacks at regular intervals during the marathon

to replenish glycogen stores, maintain blood sugar levels, and prevent bonking.
- **Hydration Stations:** Drink water or electrolyte beverages at designated hydration stations, adjusting intake based on weather conditions, sweat rate, and thirst cues to prevent dehydration and maintain electrolyte balance.

Mental Resilience and Adaptability

Draw on mental resilience techniques developed during training to overcome challenges, stay motivated, and maintain focus throughout the marathon:

- **Mantra Reinforcement:** Repeat motivational mantras or affirmations during challenging moments to stay mentally strong, redirect negative thoughts, and sustain effort towards race day goals.
- **Adaptation Strategies:** Adjust pacing, fueling, and mental strategies in response to unexpected race day variables, weather changes, or physical discomfort while maintaining confidence in your ability to navigate challenges.

Takeaway

Race day is the culmination of months of training, preparation, and anticipation, offering an opportunity to showcase your physical fitness, mental resilience, and strategic prowess as a marathoner. By optimizing morning routines, breakfast choices, warm-up exercises, and race day strategies, you can approach the starting line with confidence, execute your race plan effectively, and achieve your marathon goals with determination and satisfaction.

In the following chapters, we will explore post-marathon recovery techniques, injury prevention strategies, and reflections on the transformative impact of completing a marathon. By embracing comprehensive race day strategies, you will continue to evolve as a marathoner, setting new goals, and inspiring others through your commitment to endurance, resilience, and the pursuit of excellence.

Chapter 10: Beyond the Finish Line

Recovery and Cool Down

Crossing the marathon finish line marks the culmination of months of training, dedication, and perseverance. Effective recovery and cool down practices are essential to support physical recovery, mitigate post-race soreness, and facilitate the transition back to regular training or activities.

Immediate Post-Race Cool Down

Immediately after completing a marathon, prioritize gentle cool down activities to aid in muscle recovery, reduce stiffness, and promote circulation:

- **Walking and Light Movement:** Gradually slow down to a walk or light jog to facilitate active recovery and prevent blood pooling in fatigued muscles.
- **Stretching and Flexibility:** Perform static stretches targeting major muscle groups (e.g., quadriceps, hamstrings, calves) to alleviate tightness, improve flexibility, and promote muscle relaxation.
- **Hydration and Nutrition:** Replenish fluids with water or electrolyte beverages, consume a balanced post-race meal rich in carbohydrates, proteins, and healthy fats to support muscle repair and glycogen replenishment.

Post-Race Recovery Protocol

Implement a structured recovery protocol in the days following the marathon to promote physical recovery, optimize muscle repair, and prevent overuse injuries:

- **Active Recovery:** Engage in light cross-training activities such as swimming, cycling, or yoga to maintain aerobic fitness, enhance circulation, and alleviate muscle soreness without added impact.

- **Compression Therapy:** Use compression garments or socks to improve blood flow, reduce swelling, and expedite recovery of fatigued muscles post-marathon.
- **Massage and Foam Rolling:** Incorporate self-myofascial release techniques with foam rollers or massage tools to alleviate muscle tightness, trigger points, and promote tissue healing.
- **Sleep and Rest:** Prioritize adequate sleep and rest to facilitate recovery, support immune function, and restore energy levels depleted during marathon exertion.

Reflecting on Your Marathon Experience

Reflecting on your marathon experience provides an opportunity for personal growth, learning, and celebrating achievements while acknowledging challenges overcome along the journey:

Embracing Achievements and Milestones

Celebrate personal achievements, milestones, and the journey leading up to the marathon finish line to cultivate a sense of accomplishment and pride in your perseverance:

- **Goal Achievement:** Reflect on meeting or surpassing race day goals, whether related to finishing time, personal bests, or simply completing the marathon distance.

- **Training Progress:** Recognize improvements in fitness, endurance, and mental resilience gained through structured marathon training and consistent dedication.
- **Support Network:** Acknowledge the support of family, friends, coaches, and fellow runners who contributed to your marathon journey, fostering a sense of gratitude and community spirit.

Learning from Challenges and Setbacks

Identify and learn from challenges, setbacks, or unexpected outcomes encountered during the marathon experience to inform future training strategies and personal growth:

- **Race Day Adversities:** Analyze factors such as weather conditions, pacing strategies, nutrition/hydration issues, or physical discomforts that influenced race day performance and outcomes.
- **Adaptation and Resilience:** Reflect on moments of resilience, mental toughness, and adaptive strategies employed to overcome obstacles and maintain focus towards achieving marathon goals.

Journaling or engaging in self-reflection exercises fosters introspection, mindfulness, and deeper understanding of personal motivations, emotions, and insights gained from the marathon journey:

- **Writing Prompts:** Use writing prompts to explore thoughts, feelings, and experiences before, during, and after the marathon, capturing memories, lessons learned, and areas for growth.
- **Gratitude Practice:** Cultivate a gratitude practice by acknowledging positive aspects of the marathon experience, fostering optimism, and enhancing resilience in future challenges.

Setting New Goals

Setting new goals post-marathon sustains momentum, inspires continued progress, and reinforces commitment to ongoing personal development and achievement as a marathoner:

Goal Setting Principles

Establish SMART (Specific, Measurable, Achievable, Relevant, Time-bound) goals aligned with your evolving interests, aspirations, and long-term athletic ambitions:

- **Short-Term Objectives:** Identify immediate post-marathon goals such as recovery milestones, returning to training, or participating in shorter distance races to maintain fitness and momentum.
- **Long-Term Vision:** Define long-term goals that extend beyond the marathon, encompassing new distances, personal bests, or athletic challenges that motivate and inspire future training endeavors.
- **Non-Athletic Goals:** Consider holistic goals related to health, wellness, career, personal growth, or community involvement that complement and support your marathon journey.

Training and Race Calendar

Develop a structured training plan and race calendar that aligns with new goals, incorporating periodization, cross-training, and recovery phases to optimize performance and prevent burnout:

- **Periodization Strategy:** Divide training cycles into base building, strength development, speed work, and tapering phases to support progressive improvement and peak performance during goal races.
- **Cross-Training Benefits:** Integrate cross-training activities to enhance

overall fitness, prevent overuse injuries, and maintain motivation through diverse training modalities.
- **Race Selection:** Research and select races that challenge and align with your goals, considering factors such as course terrain, logistical considerations, and personal preferences for race experience.

Takeaway

Beyond the finish line of a marathon lies a journey of recovery, reflection, and renewed goal setting that extends the transformative impact of marathon training. By embracing structured recovery practices, reflecting on marathon achievements, and setting new goals, you continue to evolve as a marathoner, athlete, and individual committed to pursuing excellence in endurance sports and personal growth.

In the chapters ahead, we will explore injury prevention strategies, mental resilience techniques, and the enduring impact of marathon participation on physical health, well-being, and life perspective. By integrating comprehensive recovery practices and goal setting strategies into your post-marathon journey, you will continue to inspire others and cultivate a lifelong passion for running and athletic achievement.

Conclusion: Embracing Your Journey

Celebrating Your Achievement

Completing a marathon is more than crossing a finish line; it represents a culmination of dedication, perseverance, and personal growth. Celebrating your achievement is a time-honored tradition in the running community, acknowledging the milestones reached and the challenges overcome throughout your marathon journey.

Reflecting on Milestones and Progress

Take time to reflect on the milestones achieved during your marathon training and race day experience. Whether it's surpassing mileage goals, improving race times, or embracing the mental and physical challenges of long-distance running, each achievement signifies growth and resilience:

- **Training Achievements:** Recall the early mornings, the long runs in challenging weather, and the incremental improvements in fitness and endurance.
- **Race Day Highlights:** Cherish the moments of crossing the starting line, navigating through the miles, and ultimately crossing the finish line with determination and pride.

Expressing Gratitude

Express gratitude to those who supported you along your marathon journey. From family and friends to coaches, training partners, and race volunteers, their encouragement, advice, and presence contributed to your success:

- **Thank You Notes:** Consider writing thank-you notes or messages of appreciation to those who provided support, cheered you on, or helped make your marathon experience memorable.
- **Celebratory Gathering:** Organize a celebratory gathering or dinner with loved ones to share stories, laughter, and reflections on your marathon journey.

Commemorating with Memorabilia

Commemorate your marathon achievement with memorabilia such as finisher medals, race bibs, and photos capturing the essence of your marathon experience:

- **Display and Keepsakes:** Create a display or scrapbook of race memorabilia to serve as a visual reminder of your dedication, perseverance, and accomplishment.
- **Personal Reflections:** Journal about your marathon experience, capturing thoughts, emotions, and lessons learned throughout training and on race day.

Continuing Your Running Journey

Beyond the marathon finish line lies a path of continued growth, exploration, and new challenges in your running journey. Whether setting new goals, exploring different distances, or embracing running as a lifelong passion, continuing your journey enriches your life physically, mentally, and emotionally.

Setting New Goals

Setting new goals post-marathon sustains momentum and inspires ongoing progress in your running journey:

- **Short-Term Goals:** Identify immediate goals such as recovery milestones, returning to training, or participating in shorter distance races to maintain fitness and build upon your marathon success.
- **Long-Term Aspirations:** Define long-term goals that challenge and motivate you, whether aiming for new distances (e.g., ultra-marathons), setting personal bests, or exploring new running experiences.
- **Non-Athletic Goals:** Consider holistic goals related to health, wellness, career, or personal growth that complement and support your running journey.

Embracing Variety and Fun

Explore diverse running experiences to keep your journey engaging and enjoyable:

- **Trail Running:** Discover scenic trails and natural landscapes, offering varied terrain, technical challenges, and a connection with nature.
- **Community Runs:** Participate in local running events, fun runs, or themed races that foster camaraderie, community spirit, and shared passion for running.
- **Virtual Challenges:** Engage in virtual races, challenges, or group runs that provide flexibility, motivation, and opportunities to connect with runners worldwide.

Cultivating Consistency and Balance

Maintain a balanced approach to running, integrating structured training, recovery, and cross-training activities to sustain long-term progress and prevent burnout:

- **Consistent Training:** Establish a training routine that includes varied workouts (e.g., long runs, speed sessions, recovery runs) to improve fitness, performance, and overall running efficiency.
- **Cross-Training Benefits:** Incorporate cross-training activities such as swimming, cycling, or yoga to enhance cardiovascular

fitness, strength, flexibility, and injury
prevention.
- **Rest and Recovery:** Prioritize rest
  days, adequate sleep, and recovery
  techniques (e.g., foam rolling,
  massage) to optimize recovery,
  prevent overuse injuries, and maintain
  physical well-being.

Embrace the journey of running as a lifelong
pursuit of health, self-discovery, and personal
fulfillment:

- **Mindful Running:** Practice
  mindfulness techniques such as deep
  breathing, visualization, or meditation
  during runs to enhance focus, reduce
  stress, and cultivate mental resilience.
- **Social Connection:** Join running
  clubs, online communities, or local
  groups to connect with fellow runners,
  share experiences, and support each
  other's goals and achievements.
- **Inspiring Others:** Share your passion
  for running and marathon experiences
  to inspire and encourage others in
  their own fitness journeys, fostering a
  supportive and inclusive running
  community.

Final words

Completing a marathon marks a significant milestone in your running journey, reflecting dedication, perseverance, and personal growth. Celebrating your achievement acknowledges the milestones reached and the challenges overcome, while continuing your running journey sustains momentum, inspires new goals, and enriches your life with physical, mental, and emotional rewards.

As you embrace your journey beyond the marathon finish line, remember to cherish the memories, express gratitude, and set new aspirations that reflect your passion for running and commitment to personal excellence. Whether pursuing new challenges, exploring different distances, or simply enjoying the rhythm of each run, your marathon journey is a testament to resilience, determination, and the enduring spirit of a runner.

Appendix: Resources and Additional Tips

Glossary of Running Terms

Understanding key running terminology is essential for effective communication, comprehension of training plans, and navigating the marathon experience. This glossary provides definitions and explanations of commonly used running terms:

A

- **Anaerobic Threshold (AT):** The intensity of exercise at which lactate starts to accumulate in the bloodstream more quickly than it can be cleared, indicating the onset of fatigue.
- **Aerobic Capacity:** The maximum amount of oxygen the body can use during exercise; often referred to as VO2 max.
- **Arm Swing:** The movement of the arms during running, contributing to balance, rhythm, and propulsion.

B

- **Base Phase:** The initial phase of training focused on building aerobic endurance and preparing the body for more intense workouts.

- **Cadence:** The number of steps per minute while running, typically measured in strides per minute (SPM).
- **Cooldown:** Light exercise performed after a workout to gradually reduce heart rate, prevent blood pooling in muscles, and promote recovery.

C

- **Cross-Training:** Engaging in activities other than running (e.g., swimming, cycling, yoga) to complement training, improve overall fitness, and reduce injury risk.
- **Compression Gear:** Clothing designed to apply pressure to specific body parts, enhancing blood circulation, reducing muscle soreness, and aiding recovery.
- **Core Strength:** Muscular strength and endurance of the abdominals, lower back, and pelvis, essential for maintaining posture and running efficiency.

D

- **Dynamic Stretching:** Active stretching involving controlled movements through a full range of motion to improve flexibility, warm-up muscles, and prepare for exercise.
- **Drop:** The height difference between the heel and forefoot of a running

shoe; shoes with lower drops promote midfoot or forefoot striking.

E

- **Energy Gels:** Portable carbohydrate-based supplements designed to provide quick energy during endurance activities like long runs or races.
- **Elevation Gain/Loss:** The total amount of ascent (gain) or descent (loss) in a race course or training route, measured in feet or meters.

F

- **Foam Rolling:** Self-myofascial release technique using foam rollers to alleviate muscle tightness, improve flexibility, and reduce soreness.

G

- **Gait Analysis:** Assessment of a runner's biomechanics, stride pattern, and foot strike to identify inefficiencies, injury risks, and potential improvements.

H

- **Hill Repeats:** Running uphill at a challenging effort level, followed by recovery downhill or on flat terrain, to build strength, power, and cardiovascular endurance.

I

- **Interval Training:** Structured workouts involving alternating periods of high-intensity effort (work intervals) with recovery periods (rest intervals), improving speed, endurance, and aerobic capacity.

J

- **Joint Mobility:** Range of motion and flexibility of joints, crucial for running mechanics, injury prevention, and overall athletic performance.

K

- **Kinetic Chain:** The interconnected system of joints, muscles, and tendons working together to produce movement and absorb impact during running.

L

- **Lactate Threshold:** The exercise intensity at which lactate accumulation in the bloodstream increases, often used to gauge aerobic fitness and endurance capacity.

M

- **Marathon:** A road race distance of 42.195 kilometers (26.2 miles), requiring significant endurance, preparation, and mental fortitude.

N

- **Negative Splits:** Running the second half of a race faster than the first half, often associated with effective pacing and energy management strategies.

O

- **Overpronation:** Excessive inward rolling of the foot during running, potentially increasing risk of injuries like shin splints or plantar fasciitis.

P

- **Pronation:** Normal inward rolling of the foot during the running gait cycle, providing shock absorption and support for efficient propulsion.
- **Pacing:** Controlling running speed or effort level throughout a race or training session to achieve desired performance goals.

Q

- **Quad Dominance:** Overreliance on quadriceps muscles during running, potentially leading to imbalances, fatigue, or injuries without adequate strength and flexibility.

R

- **Rest Days:** Scheduled periods of complete rest from running and intense exercise to promote recovery, prevent overtraining, and optimize performance.

S

- **Strides:** Short bursts of running at faster than race pace, typically performed during warm-ups or as part of speed workouts to improve turnover and running efficiency.
- **Stability Shoes:** Running shoes designed with additional support and cushioning to reduce overpronation and enhance running gait stability.

T

- **Tapering:** Reducing training volume and intensity in the weeks leading up to a race to allow for physical and mental recovery, optimize performance, and reduce fatigue.

U

- **Ultra Marathon:** Any running race longer than the traditional marathon distance of 42.195 kilometers (26.2 miles), ranging from 50 kilometers to 100 miles or more.

V

- **VO2 Max:** Maximum volume of oxygen the body can utilize during intense exercise, often used as a measure of aerobic fitness and endurance capacity.

W

- **Warm-Up:** Preparation before running involving light aerobic activity, dynamic stretching, and drills to increase muscle temperature, joint mobility, and mental readiness.

X

- **X-Training:** Another term for cross-training, referring to engaging in alternative forms of exercise to complement running training and enhance overall fitness.

Y

- **Yasso 800s:** A workout named after Bart Yasso, involving 800-meter repeats at a pace (in minutes and seconds) that correlates with potential marathon finish time (in hours and minutes).

z

- **Zone Training:** Training based on specific heart rate zones or perceived exertion levels to optimize aerobic conditioning, endurance, and performance gains.

Sample Training Plans

Sample training plans provide structured frameworks for marathon preparation, incorporating progressive mileage, key workouts, and recovery strategies tailored to different experience levels and performance goals. These plans serve as templates for developing personalized training schedules aligned with individual needs and race objectives:

Beginner Training Plan (16-Week Program)

Week 1-4: Base Building

- **Monday:** Rest or cross-training
- **Tuesday:** 3 miles easy run
- **Wednesday:** Cross-training or rest
- **Thursday:** 3 miles easy run
- **Friday:** Rest or cross-training
- **Saturday:** 5 miles long run

- **Sunday:** Rest or recovery run (2-3 miles)

Week 5-8: Building Endurance

- **Monday:** Rest or cross-training
- **Tuesday:** 4 miles easy run
- **Wednesday:** Cross-training or rest
- **Thursday:** 4 miles easy run
- **Friday:** Rest or cross-training
- **Saturday:** 7 miles long run
- **Sunday:** Rest or recovery run (3-4 miles)

Week 9-12: Increasing Mileage

- **Monday:** Rest or cross-training
- **Tuesday:** 4 miles easy run
- **Wednesday:** Cross-training or rest
- **Thursday:** 5 miles easy run
- **Friday:** Rest or cross-training
- **Saturday:** 10 miles long run
- **Sunday:** Rest or recovery run (4-5 miles)

Week 13-16: Tapering and Race Preparation

- **Monday:** Rest or cross-training
- **Tuesday:** 4 miles easy run
- **Wednesday:** Cross-training or rest
- **Thursday:** 3 miles easy run
- **Friday:** Rest or cross-training
- **Saturday:** 8 miles long run

- **Sunday:** Rest or recovery run (2-3 miles)

Week 1-4: Base Building and Strength

- **Monday:** Rest or cross-training
- **Tuesday:** 4 miles easy run
- **Wednesday:** Cross-training or strength training
- **Thursday:** 5 miles easy run
- **Friday:** Rest or cross-training
- **Saturday:** 8 miles long run
- **Sunday:** Rest or recovery run (3 miles)

Week 5-8: Building Endurance and Speed

- **Monday:** Rest or cross-training
- **Tuesday:** 5 miles with intervals (e.g., 4x800m)
- **Wednesday:** Cross-training or strength training
- **Thursday:** 6 miles easy run
- **Friday:** Rest or cross-training
- **Saturday:** 10 miles long run
- **Sunday:** Rest or recovery run (4 miles)

Week 9-12: Increasing Mileage and Tempo Runs

- **Monday:** Rest or cross-training

- **Tuesday:** 6 miles with tempo segments
- **Wednesday:** Cross-training or strength training
- **Thursday:** 7 miles easy run
- **Friday:** Rest or cross-training
- **Saturday:** 13 miles long run
- **Sunday:** Rest or recovery run (5 miles)

Week 13-16: Peak Mileage and Race Preparation

- **Monday:** Rest or cross-training
- **Tuesday:** 7 miles with tempo segments
- **Wednesday:** Cross-training or strength training
- **Thursday:** 8 miles easy run
- **Friday:** Rest or cross-training
- **Saturday:** 16 miles long run
- **Sunday:** Rest or recovery run (6 miles)

Week 17-20: Tapering and Final Preparation

- **Monday:** Rest or cross-training
- **Tuesday:** 5 miles easy run
- **Wednesday:** Cross-training or strength training
- **Thursday:** 4 miles easy run
- **Friday:** Rest or cross-training
- **Saturday:** 10 miles long run

- **Sunday:** Rest or recovery run (3 miles)

Recommended Reading and Websites

Exploring additional resources and literature on marathon training, running techniques, and endurance sports enriches knowledge, provides diverse perspectives, and supports continuous learning and improvement:

Books

- **"Advanced Marathoning" by Pete Pfitzinger and Scott Douglas:** Comprehensive guide to marathon training principles, advanced workouts, and race day strategies.
- **"Born to Run" by Christopher McDougall:** Inspiring narrative exploring the science, culture, and endurance capabilities of human running.

Websites and Online Resources

- **Runner's World:** Offers training tips, race guides, and nutrition advice for runners of all levels.
- **Nike Run Club:** Provides personalized training plans, guided workouts, and motivational content for runners using the Nike Run Club app.

- **Strava:** Social networking platform for athletes, offering performance tracking, route planning, and community engagement features.

Podcasts

- **The Strength Running Podcast by Jason Fitzgerald:** Interviews with elite runners, coaches, and experts on training strategies, injury prevention, and mental resilience.
- **Marathon Training Academy:** Provides marathon training tips, success stories, and interviews with running professionals and athletes.

Scientific Journals

- **Journal of Science and Medicine in Sport:** Publishes research articles on sports science, exercise physiology, and performance enhancement relevant to endurance athletes.
- **Medicine & Science in Sports & Exercise (MSSE):** Official journal of the American College of Sports Medicine, featuring studies on exercise physiology, nutrition, and training methodologies.

www.ingramcontent.com/pod-product-compliance
Lightning Source LLC
Chambersburg PA
CBHW050811250726
48653CB00006B/2158